James White

A WORD to the Little Flock

Adventist Pioneer Library

© 2015 Adventist Pioneer Library

A Service of
Light Bearers Ministry
37457 Jasper Lowell Rd
Jasper, OR, 97438, USA
+1 (877) 585-1111
www.LightBearers.org
www.APLib.org

Originally published in 1847 by James S. White.

Original page numbers are in brackets.

Published in the USA

Updated May, 2015

ISBN: 978-1-61455-030-3

Table of Contents

FORWARD:
OUR PIONEERS FACING THE LIGHT

S EVENTH-DAY Adventist workers will welcome the appearance of this [...] reproduction of *A Word to the "Little Flock."* This remarkable document, issued during the critical four-year period between the Great Disappointment of October 22, 1844, and the memorable Sabbath conferences of 1848, gives an insight into the experience and thinking of our pioneers in their earnest efforts to discover their position and work and to ascertain what the future held for the believers and the world.

While this pamphlet, issued in May, 1847, contains statements signed by three early workers, James White, Ellen G. White, and Joseph Bates, it is primarily a James White publication devoted to the setting forth of his views of unfulfilled prophecy. At that time there were probably not more than one hundred Sabbath-keeping Adventists in the United States. As a youthful minister of twenty-five, he worked almost alone in setting forth the views he had, up to that time, formulated. This was nearly a year before the first of the five Sabbath conferences convened, at which time those whom we today revere as our spiritual forefathers met together and with open minds and hearts searched the Word of God to better understand its truths.

With a full understanding of the historic setting of *A Word to the "Little Flock,"* the reader will not be disturbed by finding that in a few instances positions set forth by Elder White on some points were modified by him in later years, as more mature and joint study revealed clearer views. This document presents a picture primarily of one worker's attempt to cheer and aid those about him through a dissemination of light which was beginning to unfold. To one familiar with the many contemporary voices that were heard advocating discordant views and extreme positions, the clarity of reasoning and the essential correctness of perspective and purity of teaching of these articles are remarkable.

Also of interest in this early publication are the three communications written by Mrs. E. G. White, depicting the experiences yet before the people of God. Two of these, being presentations of important visions, have been largely reprinted again and again in the E. G. White books. That some words, phrases, and sentences which appeared in these early accounts were left out by Mrs. White in later printings has been a source of concern to some. For a brief account of the first printing of these visions and a discussion of the omissions, together with Mrs. White's explanation, the reader is directed to the appendix.

That the reissuance of *A Word to the "Little Flock"* in this form, identical with its original publication, may lead to a better understanding of the experience of the founders of the message, and that it may satisfy the frequently expressed desire to have at hand for careful study, the initial E. G. White visions as first printed, is the sincere wish of the Publishers and the Trustees of the Ellen G. White Publications.

A Word to the "Little Flock"

THE following articles were written for the DAY-DAWN, which has been published at Canandaigua, New York, by O. R. L. Crosier. But as that paper is not now published, and as we do not know as it will be published again, it is thought best by some of us in Maine, to have them given in this form. I wish to call the attention of the "little flock" to those things which will very soon take place on this earth.

After our Savior had spoken of "distress of nations, with perplexity," he said, "And when these things begin to come to pass, then look up, and lift up your heads: for your redemption draweth nigh." — Luke 21:28.

We do not rejoice to know that our fellow men are distressed, and famishing for want of food: but, still, the true believer will look up, and rejoice, in view of redemption, while this sure token of the coming of the Son of Man is beginning to come to pass. When we look abroad to other nations, and see them looking to this country for food: and then look at the scarcity, and rising price of food in our own nation, we cannot doubt but that the "time of trouble such as never was," is fast coming upon the nations of the earth.

BRUNSWICK, Maine, May 30, 1847.

JAMES WHITE

THE SEVEN LAST PLAGUES

"And I saw another sign in heaven, great and marvelous, seven angels having the seven last plagues; for in them is filled up the wrath of God." — Revelation 15:1.

For more than one year, it has been my settled faith, that the seven last plagues were all in the future, and that they were all to be poured out before the first resurrection.

It may not be my duty to attempt to point out each plague separately, but only give some of my reasons for believing that they are yet to be poured out, prior to the second advent. By the light of the brightly shining lamp, (the bible) we can see the events of our past experience distinctly; while future events may not be seen in their order so clearly.

If it be true that the plagues are yet to be poured out upon the earth before the resurrection and change of the saints, has not the time fully come for us to see the light in relation to them, that we may better see, and feel the force of Christ's words? Watch ye, therefore, and pray always, that ye may be accounted worthy to escape all these things that shall come to pass, and to stand before the Son of man. Luke 21:36.

From the last clause of Revelation 15:1, "for *in them* is *filled up* the wrath of God," it seems clear that all the wrath of God to be poured out on the living wicked, is contained in the plagues. The vails of wrath will certainly be poured out, in the day of the wrath of God, and of the Lamb.

Jesus is clearly represented in the bible, in his different characters, offices, and works. At the crucifixion he was the meek, slain lamb. [2]

From the ascension, to the shutting of the door, Oct. 1844, Jesus stood with wide-spread arms of love, and mercy; ready to receive, and plead the cause of every sinner, who would come to God by him.

On the 10th day of the 7th month, 1844, he passed into the Holy of Holies, where he has since been a merciful "high priest over the house of God." But when his priestly work is finished there, he is to lay off his priestly attire, and put on his most kingly robes, to execute his judgment on the living wicked. Now where shall we look for the day of wrath, in which will be poured out the viols of wrath? Not to the crucifixion, nor while Jesus is fulfilling his Priesthood in the Heavenly Sanctuary. But, when he lays off his priestly attire, and puts on the "garments of vengeance" to "repay fury to his adversaries, recompense to his enemies;" then the day of his wrath will have fully come. As the "wrath of God" on the living wicked is *"filled up"* in the plagues, and as the day of wrath is future, it follows that the plagues are all future. I think the following is a prophesy which has been fulfilling since Oct. 1844.

"And judgment is turned away backward, and justice standeth afar off: for truth is fallen in the street, and equity cannot enter.

Yea, truth faileth; and he that departeth from evil maketh himself a prey; and the Lord saw it, and it displeased him that there was no judgment.

"And he saw that there was no man, and wondered that there was no *intercessor*." Isaiah 59:14, 15, 16.

I think that the next two verses, which speak of our Lord's putting on the "garments of vengeance for clothing," to "repay fury to his adversaries," point to the wrath of God in the seven last plagues. God has shown this day of wrath, in prophetic vision, to some of his servants by different symbols. Ezekiel saw it in the men with "slaughter-weapons," slaying "utterly, old and young." — Ezekiel 9:5, 6. John saw it in the "seven last plagues;" while Esdras saw it in the famine, pestilence, and the sword. The Bible contains many descriptions of this soon expected day of wrath.

"A thousand shall fall at thy side, and ten thousand at thy right hand; but it shall not come nigh thee" — see Psalm 91:5-10.

"Howl ye; for the day of the Lord is at hand; it shall come as a destruction from the Almighty. Therefore shall all hands be faint, and every man's heart shall melt;" — see Isaiah 13:6-11.

"And this shall be the plague wherewith the Lord will smite all the people that have fought against Jerusalem (the saints): Their flesh shall consume away while they stand upon their feet, and their eyes shall consume away in their holes, and their tongues shall consume away in their mouth." — Zechariah 14:12.

"Alas for the day! for the day of the Lord is at hand, and as a destruction from the Almighty shall it come."

"The seed is rotted under their clods, the garners are laid desolate, the barns are broken down, for the corn is withered." — see Joel 1:15-18; Jeremiah 30:23, 24; Daniel 12:1; Habakkuk 3:12, 13; Zephaniah 1:17, 18; 2 Esdras 15:10-13. I am quite sure that our Savior referred to the same, when he spake of "distress of nations, with perplexity;" "Men's hearts failing them for fear, and for looking after those things which are coming on the earth." — Luke 21:26, 27. In the 36th verse we are exhorted to constant watchfulness and prayer, that we "may be accounted worthy to escape all these things that shall come to pass, and to stand before the Son of man:" at his appearing. [3]

This makes it sure, that the trouble comes before the second advent; for the saints are to escape it, before they "stand before the Son of man." At the second appearing of our Lord Jesus Christ, the living wicked, who are not swept off by the plagues, are to be destroyed by the "brightness of his coming." — 2 Thessalonians 2:8.

This is positive proof that the plagues come before, and not after the advent; for the wicked will not suffer by the plagues, after they are destroyed by the burning glory of his coming.

The plagues of Egypt, and the deliverance of ancient Israel from bondage, clearly shadow forth the seven last plagues, and the deliverance of the saints.

"I will bring them (the saints) with a mighty hand and a stretched-out arm, and smite Egypt with plagues AS BEFORE," etc. — 2 Esdras 15:11. "Zion shall be redeemed with judgment," etc. — Isaiah 1:27. see Ezekiel 20:33-38. The plagues were poured out on Egypt just before, and at the deliverance of Israel; so we may expect the last plagues on the wicked, just before and at the deliverance of the saints.

We may see by the 91st Psalm, that many of the wicked are to be cut off, while the saints are on the earth, in their mortal state; for they are to fall by thousands all around them.

The saints are exhorted not to fear the plagues at that time, for God will give his angels charge over them, so that no plague shall come nigh their dwellings; but such an exhortation would be useless, if the saints are immortal before the plagues are poured out.

The men with slaughter-weapons in their hands have this charge, "come not near any man upon whom is the mark;" which shows that the marked saints are in their mortal state, at the slaying time.

But the humble followers of the Lamb, have nothing to fear from the terrors of the day of his wrath; for they will be sealed before the plagues are poured out.

The man "clothed with linen," marks the saints before the slaying commences.

The "four angels" are not to hurt the "earth, neither the sea, nor the trees," till the servants of God are sealed in their foreheads. — Revelation 7:1-3.

The marking or sealing of the saints, seems to be shadowed forth by the marking of the side posts and upper door posts of the houses of all Israel, before the Lord passed through Egypt, to slay the first-born of the Egyptians.

Israel was safe; for God was their protector in that perilous night. The true Israel of God will be safely protected, when Christ rules the nations with a "rod of iron," and dashes them "in pieces like a potter's vessel;" for he has promised to give his angels charge over them, to keep them in all their ways.

Those who keep the word of Christ's "patience" in this time of waiting, and trial, will then be kept "FROM the hour of temptation, (or trial) which shall come on all the WORLD, to try them that dwell upon the earth." — Revelation 3:10.

Those who do every well known duty to God, and his children: and confess their faults to God, and to one another: and are healed from their faults: will safely rest in the arms of the holy angels, while the burning wrath of God is being poured out on those who have rejected his counsel, and commandments. But I must leave this subject for the present, and close with the exhortation of the prophet:

"Seek ye the Lord, all ye meek of the earth, which have wrought [4] his judgment; seek righteousness, seek meekness: it may be ye shall be hid in the day of the Lord's anger." — Zephaniah 2:3.

THE VOICE OF GOD

"THE Lord also shall roar out of Zion, and utter his voice from Jerusalem; and the heavens and earth shall shake: but the Lord will be the hope of his people, and the strength of the children of Israel." Joel 3:16.

Second Advent writers and lecturers, have usually confounded the voice of God, which is to shake the heavens and the earth, with the "voice of the Son of God," which will call forth the saints. But I think, that we shall clearly see, that here are two distinct events. The voice of God, that is to shake the heavens and the earth, comes *"out of* Zion," and is uttered *"from* Jerusalem;" but before the voice of Jesus calls forth the sleeping saints, he is to leave the heavenly Sanctuary, and "descend *from* heaven," with his holy angels. Then, and not till then, will he send his angels to "gather his elect, from the four winds;" while his voice calls them forth to meet him "in the air." If the voice of God, which is to be uttered "from Jerusalem," raises the saints, then they will be caught up to meet the Lord in Jerusalem. But I think we shall all agree on this point, that Jesus is first to "descend from heaven" with the angels: then commission the heavenly host, to conduct the saints to meet him "in the *air*," while his voice calls them forth. — Matthew 24:30, 31. 1 Thessalonians 4:16, 17. 2 Thessalonians 1:7.

At the pouring out of the seventh vial, Revelation 16:17, we read: "and there came a great voice out of the temple of heaven, from the throne, saying, It is done." At the same time, there is a great earthquake, produced by the "voice from the throne," which shakes down the cities of the nations, and removes the islands and mountains. This "voice from the throne," which causes the earthquakes, must be the same as the voice uttered "from Jerusalem," which shakes the heavens and the earth. — Joel 3:16, and Jeremiah 25:30, 31. It seems clear that this voice which is to come *out of* the temple of heaven, *from the throne*," is not the "voice of the Son of God," that raises the saints; for if the voice that raises the saints, comes *out of* the heavenly temple, "from the throne:" then Jesus remains in heaven, on the throne, and calls his elect up to meet him in the temple; which is not in harmony with the teachings of St. Paul.

"For the Lord himself shall descend from heaven with a shout, with the voice of the arch-angel, and with the trump of God; and the dead in Christ shall rise first;

Then we, which are alive and remain, shall be caught up together with them in the clouds, to meet the Lord in the air." — 1 Thessalonians 4:16, 17. Therefore, I think we are safe, in believing that we shall hear the voice of God, which will shake the heavens and the earth, before Jesus descends from heaven, with his angels and trumpet, to awake and gather the elect in the air.

Will not the day and hour of Jesus' appearing, be made known by the voice of the Eternal God?

That the day and hour will be known by the true children of God, and no others, appears plain from the fact, that we are exhorted to watch for it; and if we do not watch, Jesus will come on us "as a thief," [5] and we shall "not know what hour" he will come upon us. So, that none but those who truly *watch*, and *"hold fast,"* will know the true time. — Revelation 3:2, 3. Here I will introduce a quotation from "The True Midnight Cry," of Aug. 22, 1844.

"Concerning the time of that (Christ's) coming, he says, in Mark 13:32, "But of that day and hour knoweth no man, no, not the angels which are in heaven, neither the Son, but the Father." It is thought by many, that this passage proves that men are never to know the time. But if it proves this, it likewise proves, that the Son of God, himself, is never to know the time; for the passage declares precisely the same concerning him, that it does concerning angels and men. But can any person believe that our glorious Lord, to whom all power in heaven and earth is given, is, and will remain ignorant of the time until the very moment that he comes to judge the world?

If not, then certainly this text can never prove that men may not be made to understand the time. An old English version of the passage, reads, "But that day and hour no man maketh known, neither the angels which are in heaven, neither the Son, but the Father."

This is the correct reading according to several of the ablest critics of the age. The word *know* is used here, in the same sense as it is by Paul in 1 Corinthians 2:2. Paul well understood many other things, besides Christ and him crucified, but he determined to *make known* nothing else among them. So in the passage first quoted, it is declared that none but God the Father, maketh known the day and hour; that is, the *definite time* of the second coming of his Son. And this necessarily implies that God makes the time known."

I believe the above, to be a fair and correct view of the subject, and that the Father will make known the true time of the advent, without the agency of men, angels, or the Son. The following prophesy is to the point.

"Son of man, what is that proverb that ye have in the land of Israel, saying, The days are prolonged, and every vision faileth?

Tell them therefore, Thus saith the Lord God; I will make this proverb to cease, and they shall no more use it as a proverb in Israel; but say unto them, The days are at hand, and the effect of every vision.

For there shall be no more any vain vision nor flattering divination within the house of Israel.

For I am the Lord: I will SPEAK, and *the word* that I shall speak shall come to pass; it shall be no more prolonged; for in your days, O rebellious house, will I SAY THE WORD, and will perform it, saith the Lord God." — Ezekiel 12:22-25.

The burden of this prophesy is time, concerning which, there has been true, and false visions. The true vision (or light) on time, was written on the Chart, or table. — Habakkuk 2:2. God approved of the proclamation of 1843, and the 10th day of the 7th month 1844: by the pouring out of the Holy Ghost. Since the 7th month 1844, the "rebellious house" of Israel, have been removing the "land-marks," and writing, and proclaiming false visions; but we all know that it has been the work of man, and not of God. These flattering divinings, have cheered on the "rebellious house" of Israel to some extent; but the work has not had the holy, sanctifying influence, as when God's hand was in the work on time.

The proverb that "every vision faileth," is, or soon will be complete; and God will make it, and the false visions to cease, by speaking from heaven, and giving his people the true time. "For I am the Lord: I [6] will SPEAK, and the word that I shall speak, shall come to pass; etc."

Now if the burden of this prophecy is time; I think all will admit, that the word that the Lord God is to speak, is the true time. The false visions that have been written, and proclaimed by the "rebellious house" of Israel, have failed: but the word to be spoken by the "Lord God," will be the true time, and will surely come to pass.

Jesus has left us the sure promise, that his Father will make known the day and the hour of his coming. The "Lord God" has promised to speak, and assures us that the word that he will speak, "shall come to pass." With such testimony as this before us, from the Father and Son, what other conclusion can we come to, than that the "word which the Father is to speak, is the true time, and when he speaks, his voice will make it known to his saints?

As the signs in the sun, moon, and stars, have been literal, the shaking of the powers of the heavens, Matthew 24:29, must also be literal.

This sign is not in the past, and as it is a sign, it must come prior to the advent itself.

Therefore, it is clear, that this last sign will appear when the "Lord roars out of Zion," and shakes the heavens and the earth. We believe that the signs in Revelation 6:12-14, are the same as in Matthew 24:29, and Mark 13:24, 25. Then the shaking of the powers of the heavens, Matthew 24:29, is the same as the heavens departing "as a scroll, when it is rolled together." Revelation 6:14· for they both follow the falling of the stars.

Now what is this heaven that is to be shaken and rolled together as a scroll? We may not see this event so clearly now, as we shall about the time of its fulfilment; but still, it is our duty to receive, and cherish all the light that we can see on this, or any other future event. As we travel onward toward the Holy City, our burning lamps discover new objects: but we cannot see all at once. If we reject a little light, because we cannot see the whole clearly at once, it will displease our heavenly leader; and we shall be left in the dark. But if we cherish the light, as fast as it is our Lord's will to open it to us, he will increase the light; and our souls will feast upon the opening truths of the blessed bible.

The word heaven, is applied to at least four places or things in the scriptures. 1st, It is applied to Paradise, where St. Paul was taken in vision, 2 Corinthians 12:2-4. 2nd. To the region of the sun, moon, and stars, Genesis 1:8-17. 3rd. To the atmosphere which encompasses this earth, in which the fowls of heaven fly. Revelation 19:17, 18. And 4th, To the church of God on earth. Revelation 14:6, 7. It cannot be Paradise, nor the region of the heavenly lights, neither the church of God on earth, that is to be shaken and rolled together as a scroll: therefore, it must be the air around the earth, in which the fowls of heaven fly.

"And the seventh angel poured out his vial into the AIR; and there came a great voice out of the temple of heaven from the throne, saying, It is done." Revelation 16:17.

We may now see that it is the seventh vial, and voice of God, which will shake the powers of the heavens, and cause the great earthquake or the shaking of the earth: and that this event constitutes the last literal sign, just before the sign of the Son of man appears in heaven.

It seems clear that all the vials, the voice of God from the throne, the voices, and thunders, and lightnings, and the great earthquake, and the falling of the cities of the nations, and the removing of the mountains and the islands, are to take place before the advent. [7]

This view no doubt, will at once be rejected by many who profess to be looking for Jesus every day and hour; but I think it will appear very plain, by comparing Revelation 16:17-21, with chap. 6:14-17.

After the heavens depart "as a scroll when rolled together," and the "mountains and islands are moved out of their places," "the kings of the earth, and great men, etc." "hide in the dens, and in the rocks of the mountains," from the awful glory of the coming Jesus, attended by "all the holy angels;" and call for the rocks and mountains to fall on them, and hide them from the *brightness of his coming* (which is to destroy all the living wicked at his coming. — 2 Thessalonians 2:8.); and overwhelmed with anguish, in view of their expected fate, (when Christ and the angels draw near the earth to raise and gather the elect,) they cry out: "For the great day of his wrath is come, and who shall be able to stand?" — Revelation 6:17.

Here we see that the wicked who are hid, are still looking forward to the time when the saints alone will "be able to stand" before Christ at his appearing. If Christ should burst in upon the world as suddenly and unexpectedly as some teach, no one would think of hiding in caves, dens, and rocks: for they are not within their reach. This shows that an entire change must take place in the earth's surface prior to the second advent, by the voice of God, in order for the wicked to have a chance to hide from the expected Lamb, in caves, dens, and rocks of the mountains. When the Father utters his voice "from the throne," which is to cause "a great earthquake, such as was not since men were upon the earth:" then there will be a chance for all the wicked, who are not swept off by the former plagues, to hide from the presence of the Lamb. But rocks, caves, and dens, will not shelter them from the burning glory of that holy throng, for all the living wicked are to be destroyed "with the brightness of that coming." — 2 Thessalonians 2:8.

God has promised to be the "hope of his people," at the time his voice shakes the heavens and the earth. His children have nothing to fear from the terrors of that day; for they will be sheltered from the falling of cities, mountains, and houses. God's promise cannot fail.

That will be a glad day for the saints; for they will then be "delivered" from every outward foe, and be filled with the Holy Ghost, to prepare them to gaze on Jesus, and stand before him at his appearing. Then the saints will better know the real worth of the blessed hope; and they will rejoice that they have been accounted worthy to suffer reproach for clinging close to the truth, and strictly obeying all the "commandments of God." When God spake to Moses in Sinai, his "voice then shook the earth;" and we are taught by St. Paul, in Hebrews 12:22-27, that he is yet to speak from the "City of the living God," and "shake not only the earth, but also heaven." When God spake to Moses, the glory rested on him so that he had to cover his face with a vail, before his brethren could stand before him, and hear the word of the Lord from his mouth. And may we not expect the same effect, from the same cause? If so, then when God speaks from the Holy City to all his people, as he did to Moses: all will have the glory poured on them, as Moses had it poured on him. This out-pouring of the Holy Ghost must take place before the second advent, to prepare us for the glory of that scene: for in our present state, none of us could stand a single moment before the brightness of that coming, which is to destroy the "man of sin." At the presence of one angel at the resurrection of Christ, the Roman guard fell like dead men to the ground. It is therefore necessary, that the saints should share largely in the [8] glory of God, to prepare them to stand before the Son of God, when he comes with all the holy angels with him.

Our present trying, waiting, watching state, is represented by a dark night; and the coming glory before us, by the morning. There are two parts to the morning: first, the dawn of day, and second, full day light, which is completed by the rising of the sun. So in the glad morning before us; the day of rest will dawn at the voice of God, when his light, and glory, rest upon us; then we shall rise from glory to glory, till Christ appears, to clothe us with immortality, and give us eternal life. O, Glory! Hallelujah!! my poor heart is set on fire for the kingdom, while I dwell on this sweet prospect, before the true believer. If we "hold fast" but a few days more, the dark shades of night will vanish before the glory of the preparatory scenes of the coming of the Son of man.

THE TIME OF TROUBLE

"AND at that time shall Michael stand up, the great prince which standeth for the children of thy people: and there shall be a time of trouble, such as never was since there was a nation even to that same time: and at that time thy people shall be delivered, every one that shall be found written in the book. And many of them that sleep in the dust of the earth shall awake," etc. — Daniel 12:1, 2.

We are taught by some, that the standing up of Michael, the time of trouble, and the delivering of the saints are in the future; and that all these events are to be accomplished at the second appearing of Christ. Others teach, that Michael stood up on the 10th day of the 7th month, 1844, and that since that time we have been passing through the "time of trouble, such as never was;" and that the deliverance of the saints, is at the first resurrection. But as I cannot harmonize either of these views with the bible, I wish to humbly give my brethren and sisters my view of these events. It is clear to me, that here are four distinct events, all in the future. 1st. The standing up of Michael. 2nd. The time of trouble. 3rd. The deliverance of the saints; and 4th. The resurrection of the just, to everlasting life.

That Jesus rose up, and shut the door, and came to the Ancient of days, to receive his kingdom, at the 7th month, 1844, I fully believe. See Luke 13:25; Matthew 25:10; Daniel 7:13, 14. But the standing up of Michael, Daniel 12:1, appears to be another event, for another purpose. His rising up in 1844, was to shut the door, and come to his Father, to receive his kingdom, and power to reign; but Michael's standing up, is to manifest his kingly power, which he already has, in the destruction of the wicked, and in the deliverance of his people. Michael is to stand up at the time that the last power in chap. 11, comes to his end, and none to help him. This power is the last that treads down the true church of God: and as the true church is still trodden down, and cast out by all christendom, it [9] follows that the last oppressive power has not "come to his end;" and Michael has not stood up. This last power that treads down the saints is brought to view in Revelation 13:11-18. His number is 666. Much of his power, deception, wonders, miracles, and oppression, will doubtless be manifested during his last struggle under the "seven last plagues," about the time of his coming to his end. This is clearly shadowed forth by the magicians of Egypt, deceiving Pharaoh and his host, in performing most of the miracles, that Moses performed by the power of God. That was just before the deliverance of Israel from Egyptian bondage; and may we not expect to see as great a manifestation of the power of the Devil, just before the glorious deliverance of the saints? If Michael stood up in 1844, what power came "to his end, and none to help him," "AT THAT TIME"? The trouble that is to come at the time that Michael stands up, is not the trial, or trouble of the saints; but it is a trouble of the nations of the earth, caused by "seven last plagues." So when Jesus has finished his work of atonement, in the Holy of Holies, he will lay off his priestly attire, and put on his most kingly robes and crown, to ride forth, and manifest his kingly power, in ruling the nations, and dashing them in pieces.

We believe, that our great High Priest is attired as the Jewish high priest was. See Leviticus 16c. But when Michael stands up to reign, KING OF KINGS, AND LORD OF LORDS, he has on, many crowns, in one crown. Revelation 19:16.

The deliverance of the living saints, is before the first resurrection; for it is spoken of, as a separate event.

If the deliverance of the living saints is not until the first resurrection; why is the resurrection spoken of, as a separate event, after the deliverance? It seems clear that the deliverance is at the voice of God. Then, from that time till Christ appears, the saints will have power over the nations, who remain of the former plagues.

THE TIME OF JACOB'S TROUBLE

"ALAS! for that day is great, so that none is like it; it is even the time of Jacob's trouble, but he shall be saved out of it." Jeremiah 30:7.

By comparing Gen. c. 32, with Jeremiah 30:7, and the prophesy of Obadiah, we may see that Jacob represents believers, and Esau represents unbelievers. I doubt not, but these two characters will be brought out, and clearly seen in the closing strife with the Image Beast, which is just before us. See Revelation 13:11-18. Jacob's trouble was when the messengers returning to him, said, "We came to thy brother Esau, and also he cometh to meet thee, and four hundred men with him. Then Jacob was greatly afraid, and distressed." Genesis 32:6, 7.

The true saints will be brought into a similar situation, at the time of the fulfilment of Revelation 13:11-18. [10]

Not that the saints will be killed; for then none would remain till the change: but to fulfil this prophesy, a decree must go forth to kill the saints, which will cause fear, and distress. When Jacob was troubled, he wrestled with the angels "until the breaking of the day." Genesis 32:24. In the last closing strife with the Image Beast, when a decree goes forth that as many as will not worship the image of the beast shall "be killed," the saints will cry day and night, and be delivered by the voice of God. Then "the house of Jacob shall be a fire, and the house of Joseph a flame, and the house of Esau for stubble, and they shall kindle in them, and devour them, and there shall not be any remaining of the house of Esau; for the Lord hath spoken it." Obadiah 18th verse. I have not been able to see any thing in our past and present history, which answers to Jacob's trouble, and the day and night cry of the elect. Luke 17:7. I have been astonished at some of our brethren, while they have urged us to go about the work of crying day and night for deliverance. Not long since, I was in a meeting where the sentiment prevailed, that if all would then go about the work they might pray Christ down to the earth in twenty-four hours. It is clear that when the time comes for this cry, that the elect will have the spirit of prayer poured upon them. "And I will pour upon the house of David, and upon the inhabitants of Jerusalem, the spirit of grace and supplication," etc. "And the land shall mourn, every family apart; the family of the house of David apart, and their wives apart;" See Zechariah 12:14; Ezekiel 7:15, 16.

When Jesus has finished his work in the Heavenly Sanctuary and comes out upon the great white cloud, with his sharp sickle, then will be the time for the day and night cry, which is represented by the angel's crying to Jesus, to thrust in his sharp sickle, and reap. — Revelation 14:14, 15.

The desire, and prayer of every pure soul is, "Thy kingdom come." But the special mourning, praying time of the saints, is evidently yet to come.

THOUGHTS ON REVELATION 14

THE 13th chapter of Revelation, and the first five verses of the 14th, is one connected chain of past, present, and future events, down to the complete redemption of the 144000: then the 6th verse commences another chain of events, which carry us down through the history of God's people in this mortal state. John had a view of the beast and his image, as recorded in chapter 13th; and how natural it would be for him to view on a little further, and see the 144000, who had gotten the victory over the beast, and over his image, standing on mount Zion with the Lamb, etc., as recorded in chapter 14:1-5. So I think the division should be between the 5th, and 6th verses of the 14th chapter; and the 6th verse commences a series of events, relative to the successive messages of holy advent truth.

All classes of second advent believers agree, that the angel brought to view in the 6th, and 7th verses of this chapter, represents [11] the advent message, to the church and world. If this is true, then all five of the angels brought to view in this chapter, represent five distinct messages, prior to the advent, or we are left without a rule to interpret this chapter.

The work of the second angel, was to show to the advent host that Babylon had fallen. And as a large portion of them did not learn this fact, until the power of the MIDNIGHT CRY waked them up, just in time for them to make their escape from the churches, before the 10th day came on; it follows, that the second angel brought us to the 7th month, 1844. The third angel's message was, and still is, a WARNING to the saints to "hold fast," and not go back, and "receive" the marks which the virgin band got rid of, during the second angel's cry.

And has not the true message for God's people, since the 7th month 1844, been just such a warning? It certainly has. I cannot agree with those who make two messages of the cry, "Babylon the great, is fallen," and the voice, "Come out of her my people"; for every sermon that was printed, or preached on this subject, contained them both in one message. The 12th verse reads, "Here is the patience of the saints: here are they that keep the commandments of God," etc. Where did you see them, John? Why, *"here"* during this third angel. As the patient waiting time has been since the 7th month 1844, and as the class that keep the sabbath, etc. have appeared since that time: it is plain that we live in the time of the third angel's message.

The last two angels are messages of prayer. We shall, no doubt, better understand them at the time of their fulfilment.

JAMES WHITE.

TOPSHAM, April 21, 1847.

To Bro. ELI CURTIS, New York City.

Dear Bro:—In the Day-Dawn, Vol. 1, Nos. 10 and 11, you kindly invite me to address you a communication.

The only apology I have to offer for not writing before is, I have not had a clear duty to write till now. You will, I doubt not, excuse me for addressing you so publicly, at this time. I have been much interested in your writings in the Dawn, and Extra; and fully agree with you on some points, but on others we widely differ.

Your Extra is now on the stand before me; and I beg leave to state to you, and the scattered flock of God, what I have seen in vision relative to these things on which you have written. I fully agree with you, that there will be two literal resurrections, 1000 years apart.

I also agree with you, that the new heavens, and the new earth, (Revelation 21:1. Isaiah 65:17. 2 Peter 3:13.) will not appear, till after the wicked dead are raised, and destroyed, at the end of the 1000 years. I saw that Satan was "loosed out of his prison," at the end of the 1000 years, just at the time the wicked dead were raised; and that Satan deceived them by making them believe that they could take the Holy City from [12] the saints. The wicked all marched up around the "camp of the saints," with Satan at their head; and when they were ready to make an effort to take the City, the Almighty breathed from his high throne, on the City, a breath of devouring fire, which came down on them, and burnt them up, "root and branch."

And I saw, that as Christ is the vine, and his children the branches: so Satan is the "root", and his children are the "branches;" and at the final destruction of "Gog and Magog," the whole wicked host will be burnt up, "root and branch," and cease to exist. Then will appear the new heaven and the new earth. Then will the saints "build houses," and "plant vineyards." I saw, that all the righteous dead were raised by the voice of the Son of God, at the first resurrection; and all that were raised at the second resurrection, were burnt up, and ceased to exist.

You think, that those who worship before the saint's feet, (Revelation 3:9), will at last be saved. Here I must differ with you; for God shew me that this class were professed Adventists, who had fallen away, and "crucified to themselves the Son of God afresh, and put him to an open shame." And in the "hour of temptation," which is yet to come, to show out every one's true character, they will know that they are forever lost; and overwhelmed with anguish of spirit, they will bow at the saint's feet.

You also think, that Michael stood up, and the time of trouble commenced, in the spring of 1844.

The Lord has shown me in vision, that Jesus rose up, and shut the door, and entered the Holy of Holies, at the 7th month 1844; but Michael's standing up (Daniel 12:1) to deliver his people, is in the future.

This, will not take place, until Jesus has finished his priestly office in the Heavenly Sanctuary, and lays off his priestly attire, and puts on his most kingly robes, and crown, to ride forth on the cloudy chariot, to "thresh the heathen in anger," and deliver his people.

Then Jesus will have the sharp sickle in his hand, (Revelation 14:14) and then the saints will cry day and night to Jesus on the cloud, to thrust in his sharp sickle and reap.

This, will be the time of Jacob's trouble, (Jeremiah 30:5-8) out of which, the saints will be delivered by the voice of God.

I believe the Sanctuary, to be cleansed at the end of the 2300 days, is the New Jerusalem Temple, of which Christ is a minister. The Lord shew me in vision, more than one year ago, that Brother Crosier had the true light, on the cleansing of the Sanctuary, etc; and that it was his will, that Brother C. should write out the view which he gave us in the Day-Star, Extra, February 7, 1846. I feel fully authorized by the Lord, to recommend that Extra, to every saint.

I pray that these lines may prove a blessing to you, and all the dear children who may read them.

E. G. WHITE. [13]

"And it shall come to pass in the last days, saith God, I will pour out of my Spirit upon all flesh: and your sons and your daughters shall prophesy, and your young men shall see Visions, and your old men shall dream dreams: And on my servants, and on my hand-maidens, I will pour out in those days of my Spirit;

and they shall prophesy: And I will shew wonders in heaven above, and signs in the earth beneath; blood and fire and vapor of smoke. The sun shall be turned into darkness, and the moon into blood, before that great and notable day of the Lord come". Acts 2:17-20.

"When the day of Pentecost was fully come," and the disciples were "all with one accord in one place," filled with the Holy Ghost, "Peter standing up with the eleven," quoted the above scripture from the prophesy of Joel. His object was to show that the marvelous work which was wrought in the disciples at that time, was a subject of prophesy, and the work of God. I conclude that there is not one Second Advent believer who will take the ground, that all of the prophesy of Joel, quoted by Peter, was fulfilled on the day of Pentecost; for there is not the least evidence that any part of it was then fulfilled, only that part which related to the pouring out of the Holy Ghost. We cannot believe that the signs in the sun, and the moon, etc, were seen on that day, or that there were any having visions, or dreaming among them at that exciting hour; for there is no proof of any such thing. A part of this prophesy was fulfilled on the day of Pentecost; and ALL of it is to be fulfilled "IN THE LAST DAYS, SAITH GOD." Dreams and Visions are among the signs that precede the great and notable days of the Lord. And as the signs of that day have been, and still are fulfilling, it must be clear to every unprejudiced mind, that the time has fully come, when the children of God may expect dreams and visions from the Lord.

I know that this is a very unpopular position to hold on this subject, even among Adventists; but I choose to believe the word of the Lord on this point, rather than the teachings of men. I am well aware of the prejudice in many minds on this subject; but as it has been caused principally by the preaching of popular Adventists, and the lack of a correct view of this subject;

I have humbly hoped to cut it away, with the "sword of the Spirit," from some minds, at least. We will bear it in mind, that these dreams and visions, are to be in the "LAST DAYS". As there cannot be any days later than the last, it is certain that we may expect just such revelations, until Christ appears in the clouds of heaven. I know that it is a very popular opinion among Adventists, that there was nothing more to be revealed by visions, after John closed up the revelation in A. D. 96. But if this opinion is correct, then the last days ended while John was on the isle of Patmos.

The bible is a perfect, and complete revelation. It is our only rule of faith and practice. But this is no reason, why God may not show the past, present, and future fulfilment of his word, in these *last days*, by dreams and visions; according to Peter's testimony. True visions are given to lead us to God, and his written word; but those that are given for a new rule of faith and practice, separate from the bible, cannot be from God, and should be rejected.

The following vision was published in the Day-Star, more than a year ago. By the request of friends, it is republished in this little work, with scripture references, for the benefit of the little flock.

I hope that all who may read it, will take the wise, and safe course, pointed out to us by the following passages of scripture. "Despise not [14] prophesyings. Prove all things; hold fast that which is good." Paul. "To the law and to the testimony, if they speak not according to this word, it is because there is no light in them." Isaiah 8:20.

TO THE REMNANT
SCATTERED ABROAD

As God has shown me in holy vision the travels of the Advent people to the Holy City, and the rich reward to be given those who wait the return of their Lord from the wedding, it may be my duty to give you a short sketch of what God has revealed to me. The dear saints have got many trials to pass through. But our light afflictions, which are but for a moment, worketh for us a far more exceeding and eternal weight of glory — while we look not at the things which are seen, for the things which are seen are temporal, but the things which are not seen are eternal. I have tried to bring back a good report, and a few grapes from the heavenly Canaan, for which many would stone me, as the congregation bade stone Caleb and Joshua for their report, (Numbers 14:10.) But I declare to you, my brethren and sisters in the Lord, it is a goodly land, and we are well able to go up and possess it.

While praying at the family altar, the Holy Ghost fell on me, and I seemed to be rising higher and higher, far above the dark world. I turned to look for the Advent people in the world, but could not find them — when a voice said to me, "Look again, and look a little higher." At this I raised my eyes and saw a straight and narrow path,[1] cast up high above the world. On this path the Advent people were travelling to the City, which was at the farther end of the path. They had a bright light set up

---

[1] Matthew 7:14.

behind them at the first end of the path, which an angel told me was the Midnight Cry.[2] This light shone all along the path, and gave light for their feet so they might not stumble. And if they kept their eyes fixed on Jesus, who was just before them, leading them to the City, they were safe. But soon some grew weary, and they said the City was a great way off, and they expected to have entered it before. Then Jesus would encourage them by raising his glorious right arm, and from his arm came a glorious light which waved over the Advent band, and they shouted Hallelujah! Others rashly denied the light behind them, and said that it was not God that had led them out so far. The light behind them went out leaving their feet in perfect darkness, and they stumbled and got their eyes off the mark and lost sight of Jesus, and fell off the path down in the dark and wicked world below. It was just as impossible for them to get on the path again and go to the City, as all the wicked world which God had rejected. They fell all the way along the path one after another, until we heard the voice of God like many waters,[3] which gave us the day and hour of Jesus' coming.[4] The living saints, 144,000 in number, knew and understood the voice, while the wicked thought it was thunder and an earthquake.[5] When God spake the time, he poured on us the Holy Ghost, and our faces began to light up and shine with the glory of God as Moses' did when he came down from Mount Sinai.[6]

By this time the 144,000 were all sealed and perfectly united. On their foreheads was written, God, New Jerusalem, and a glorious Star containing Jesus' new name.[7] At our happy,

---

[2] Matthew 25:6.
[3] Ezekiel 43:2. Joel 3:16. Revelation 16:17.
[4] Ezekiel 12:25. Mark 13:32.
[5] John 12:29.
[6] Isaiah 10:27.
[7] Revelation 3:12.

holy state the wicked [15] were enraged, and would rush violently up to lay hands on us to thrust us in prison, when we would stretch forth the hand in the name of the Lord, and the wicked would fall helpless to the ground. Then it was that the synagogue of Satan knew that God had loved us who could wash one another's feet, and salute the holy brethren with a holy kiss, and they worshipped at our feet.[8] Soon our eyes were drawn to the East, for a small black cloud had appeared about half as large as a man's hand, which we all knew was the Sign of the Son of Man.[9] We all in solemn silence gazed on the cloud as it drew nearer, lighter, and brighter, glorious, and still more glorious, till it was a great white cloud.[10] The bottom appeared like fire, a rainbow was over it, around the cloud were ten thousand angels singing a most lovely song. And on it sat the Son of Man,[11] on his head were crowns,[12] his hair was white and curly and lay on his shoulders.[13] His feet had the appearance of fire,[14] in his right hand was a sharp sickle,[15] in his left a silver trumpet.[16] His eyes were as a flame of fire,[17] which searched his children through and through. Then all faces gathered paleness, and those that God had rejected gathered blackness. Then we all cried out, who shall be able to stand? Is my robe spotless? Then the angels ceased to sing, and there was some time of awful silence,[18] when Jesus spoke. Those who have clean hands and a pure heart shall

---

[8] Revelation 3:9.
[9] Matthew 24:30.
[10] Revelation 14:14.
[11] Luke 21:27.
[12] Revelation 19:12.
[13] Revelation 1:14.
[14] Revelation 1:15.
[15] Revelation 14:14.
[16] 1 Thessalonians 4:16.
[17] Revelation 1:14.
[18] Revelation 8:1.

be able to stand, my grace is sufficient for you. At this, our faces lighted up, and joy filled every heart. And the angels struck a note higher and sung again while the cloud drew still nearer the earth. Then Jesus' silver trumpet sounded, as he descended on the cloud, wrapped in flames of fire.[19] He gazed on the graves of the sleeping saints, then raised his eyes and hands to heaven and cried out,[20] Awake! Awake! Awake! ye that sleep in the dust, and arise. Then there was a mighty earthquake. The graves opened, and the dead came up clothed with immortality. The 144,000 shouted, Hallelujah! as they recognized their friends who had been torn from them by death, and in the same moment we were changed and caught up together with them to meet the Lord in the air.[21] We all entered the cloud together, and were seven days ascending to the sea of glass, when Jesus brought along the crowns and with his own right hand placed them on our heads.[22] He gave us harps of gold and palms of victory.[23] Here on the sea of glass the 144,000 stood in a perfect square. Some of them had very bright crowns, others not so bright. Some crowns appeared heavy with stars, while others had but few. All were perfectly satisfied with their crowns. And they were all clothed with a glorious white mantle from their shoulders to their feet.[24] Angels were all about us as we marched over the sea of glass to the gate of the City. Jesus raised his mighty glorious arm, laid hold of the gate and swung it back on its golden hinges, and said to us, You have washed your robes in my blood, stood stiffly for my truth, enter in.[25] We all marched in and felt we had a perfect right in the City. Here we saw the tree of life, and the

---

[19] 2 Thessalonians 1:7, 8.

[20] 1 John 5:25.

[21] 1 Thessalonians 4:17.

[22] 2 Esdras 2:43

[23] Revelation 15:2. Revelation 7:9.

[24] Revelation 7:9.

[25] Isaiah 26:2.

throne of God. Out of the throne came a pure river of water, and on either side of the river was the tree of life.[26] On one side of the river was a trunk of a tree and a trunk on the other side of the river, both of pure transparent gold. [16]

At first I thought I saw two trees. I looked again and saw they were united at the top in one tree. So it was the tree of life, on either side of the river of life; its branches bowed to the place where we stood; and the fruit was glorious, which looked like gold mixed with silver. We all went under the tree, and sat down to look at the glory of the place, when brothers Fitch and Stockman, who had preached the gospel of the kingdom, and whom God had laid in the grave to save them, came up to us and asked us what we had passed through while they were sleeping. We tried to call up our greatest trials, but they looked so small compared with the far more exceeding and eternal weight of glory[27] that surrounded us, that we could not speak them out,[28] and we all cried out Hallelujah, heaven is cheap enough, and we touched our glorious harps and made heaven's arches ring. And as we were gazing at the glories of the place our eyes were attracted upwards to something that had the appearance of silver. I asked Jesus to let me see what was within there. In a moment we were winging our way upward, and entering in; here we saw good old father Abraham, Isaac, Jacob, Noah, Daniel, and many like them. And I saw a vail with a heavy fringe of silver and gold, as a border on the bottom; it was very beautiful. I asked Jesus what was within the vail. He raised it with his own right arm, and bade me take heed. I saw there a glorious ark, overlaid with pure gold, and it had a glorious border, resembling Jesus' crowns; and on it were two bright angels — their wings were spread over the ark as they sat on each end, with their faces turned towards

---

[26] Revelation 22:1, 2.
[27] 2 Corinthians 4:17.
[28] Isaiah 65:17.

each other and looking downward.[29] In the ark, beneath where the angels' wings were spread, was a golden pot of Manna, of a yellowish cast; and I saw a rod, which Jesus said was Aaron's; I saw it bud, blossom and bear fruit.[30] And I saw two long golden rods, on which hung silver wires, and on the wires most glorious grapes; one cluster was more than a man here could carry. And I saw Jesus step up and take of the manna, almonds, grapes and pomegranates, and bear them down to the city, and place them on the supper table. I stepped up to see how much was taken away, and there was just as much left; and we shouted Hallelujah — Amen. We all descended from this place down into the city, and with Jesus at our head we all descended from the city down to this earth, on a great and mighty mountain, which could not bear Jesus up, and it parted asunder, and there was a mighty plain.[31] Then we looked up and saw the great city, with twelve foundations, twelve gates, three on each side, and an angel at each gate, and all cried out, "the city, the great city, it's coming, it's coming down from God, out of heaven;"[32] and it came and settled on the place where we stood. Then we began to look at the glorious things outside of the city. There I saw most glorious houses, that had the appearance of silver, supported by four pillars, set with pearls, most glorious to behold, which were to be inhabited by the saints;[33] in them was a golden shelf; I saw many of the saints go into the houses, take off their glittering crowns and lay them on the shelf, then go out into the field by the houses to do something with the earth;[34] not as we have to do with the earth here; no, no. A glorious light shone all about

---

[29] Exodus 25:18, 20. Hebrews 9:3-5.

[30] Numbers 17:8.

[31] Zechariah 14:4.

[32] Revelation 21:10-13.

[33] Isaiah 65:21.

[34] Isaiah 65:21.

their heads, and they were continually shouting and offering praises to God. [17]

And I saw another field full of all kinds of flowers, and as I plucked them, I cried out, well they will never fade. Next I saw a field of tall grass, most glorious to behold; it was living green, and had a reflection of silver and gold, as it waved proudly to the glory of King Jesus. Then we entered a field full of all kinds of beasts — the lion, the lamb, the leopard and the wolf, altogether in perfect union;[35] we passed through the midst of them, and they followed on peaceably after. Then we entered a wood, not like the dark woods we have here, no, no; but light, and all over glorious; the branches of the trees waved to and fro, and we all cried out, "we will dwell safely in the wilderness and sleep in this woods."[36] We passed through the woods, for we were on our way to Mount Zion. As we were travelling along, we met a company who were also gazing at the glories of the place. I noticed red as a border on their garments; their crowns were brilliant; their robes were pure white. As we greeted them, I asked Jesus who they were? He said they were martyrs that had been slain for him. With them was an innumerable company of little ones; they had a hem of red on their garments also.[37] Mount Zion was just before us, and on the Mount sat a glorious temple, and about it were seven other mountains, on which grew roses and lillies,[38] and I saw the little ones climb, or if they chose, use their little wings and fly to the top of the mountains, and pluck the never fading flowers. There were all kinds of trees around the temple to beautify the place; the box, the pine, the fir, the oil, the myrtle, the pomegranate, and the fig tree bowed down with the weight of its timely figs, that made the place

---

[35] Isaiah 11:6-9.
[36] Ezekiel 34:25.
[37] Jeremiah 31:15-17. Matthew 2:18.
[38] 2 Esdras 2:19.

look all over glorious.[39] And as we were about to enter the holy temple, Jesus raised his lovely voice and said, only the 144,000 enter this place, and we shouted Hallelujah.

Well, bless the Lord, dear brethren and sisters, it is an extra meeting for those who have the seal of the living God.[40] This temple was supported by seven pillars, all of transparent gold, set with pearls most glorious. The glorious things I saw there, I cannot describe to you. O, that I could talk in the language of Canaan, then could I tell a little of the glory of the upper world; but, if faithful, you soon will know all about it. I saw there the tables of stone in which the names of the 144,000 were engraved in letters of gold; after we had beheld the glory of the temple, we went out. Then Jesus left us, and went to the city; soon, we heard his lovely voice again, saying — "Come my people, you have come out of great tribulation, and done my will; suffered for me; come in to supper, for I will gird myself, and serve you."[41] We shouted Hallelujah, glory, and entered into the city.... ....And I saw a table of pure silver, it was many miles in length, yet our eyes could extend over it. And I saw the fruit of the tree of life, the manna, almonds, figs, pomegranates, grapes, and many other kinds of fruit. We all reclined at the table. I asked Jesus to let me eat of the fruit. He said, not now. Those who eat of the fruit of this land, go back to earth no more. But in a little while, if faithful, you shall both eat of the fruit of the tree of life, and drink of the water of the fountain; and he said, you must go back to the earth again, and relate to others, what I have revealed to you. Then an angel bore me gently down to this dark [18] world. Sometimes I think I cannot stay here any longer, all things of earth look so dreary —

---

[39] Isaiah 60:13. Isaiah 41:19.
[40] Revelation 14:3.
[41] Luke 12:37.

I feel very lonely here, for I have seen a better land. O, that I had wings like a dove, then would I fly away, and be at rest.

TOPSHAM, Me., April 7, 1847.

Dear Brother Bates:—Last Sabbath we met with the dear brethren and sisters here, who meet at Bro. Howland's.

We felt an unusual spirit of prayer. And as we prayed, the Holy Ghost fell upon us. We were very happy. Soon I was lost to earthly things, and was wrapped up in a vision of God's glory. I saw an angel swiftly flying to me. He quickly carried me from the earth to the Holy City. In the city I saw a temple, which I entered. I passed through a door before I came to the first vail. This vail was raised, and I passed into the Holy Place. Here I saw the Altar of Incense, the candlestick with seven lamps, and the table on which was the showbread, etc. After viewing the glory of the Holy, Jesus raised the second veil, and I passed into the Holy of Holies.[42]

In the Holiest I saw an ark; on the top and sides of it was purest gold. On each end of the ark was a lovely Cherub, with their wings spread out over it. Their faces were turned towards each other, and they looked downwards.[43] Between the angels was a golden censor. Above the ark, where the angels stood, was an exceeding bright glory, that appeared like a throne where God dwelt.[44] Jesus stood by the ark. And as the saints' prayers came up to Jesus, the incense in the censor would smoke, and He offered up the prayers of the saints with the smoke of the incense to His Father.[45] In the ark, was the golden pot of manna, Aaron's rod that budded, and the tables of stone which

---

[42] Hebrews 9:1-24.

[43] Exodus 25:18-22.

[44] Exodus 25:20-22.

[45] Revelation 8: 3, 4.

folded together like a book.[46] Jesus opened them, and I saw the ten commandments written on them with the finger of God.[47] On one table was four, and on the other six. The four on the first table shone brighter than the other six. But the fourth (the Sabbath commandment,) shone above them all; for the Sabbath was set apart to be kept in honor of God's holy name.[48] The holy Sabbath looked glorious — a halo of glory was all around it. I saw that the Sabbath was not nailed to the cross. If it was, the other nine commandments were; and we are at liberty to go forth and break them all, as well as to break the fourth. I saw that God had not changed the Sabbath, for He never changes.[49] But the Pope had changed it from the seventh to the first day of the week; for he was to change times and laws.[50]

And I saw that if God had changed the Sabbath, from the seventh to the first day, He would have changed the writing of the Sabbath commandment, written on the tables of stone, which are now in the ark, in the Most Holy Place of the Temple in heaven;[51] and it would read thus: The first day is the [19] Sabbath of the Lord thy God. But I saw that it read the same as when written on the tables of stone by the finger of God, and delivered to Moses in Sinai, "But the seventh day is the Sabbath of the Lord thy God."[52] I saw that the holy Sabbath is, and will be, the separating wall between the true Israel of God and unbelievers; and that the Sabbath is the great question, to unite the hearts of God's dear waiting saints. And if one believed, and kept the Sabbath, and received the blessing attending it, and then gave it up, and broke the holy commandment, they would

---

[46] Hebrews 9:4.

[47] Exodus 31:18.

[48] Isaiah 58:13, 14.

[49] Malachi 3:6.

[50] Daniel 7:25.

[51] Revelation 11:19.

[52] Exodus 20:10.

shut the gates of the Holy City against themselves, as sure as there was a God that rules in heaven above. I saw that God had children, who do not see and keep the Sabbath. They had not rejected the light on it. And at the commencement of the time of trouble, we were filled with the Holy Ghost as we went forth[53] and proclaimed the Sabbath more fully. This enraged the church, and nominal Adventists, as they could not refute the Sabbath truth. And at this time, God's chosen, all saw clearly that we had the truth, and they came out and endured the persecution with us. And I saw the sword, famine, pestilence, and great confusion in the land.[54] The wicked thought that we had brought the judgments down on them. They rose up and took counsel to rid the earth of us, thinking that then the evil would be stayed.[55]

I saw all that "would not receive the mark of the Beast, and of his Image, in their foreheads or in their hands," could not buy or sell.[56] I saw that the number (666) of the Image Beast was made up;[57] and that it was the beast that changed the Sabbath, and the Image Beast had followed on after, and kept the Pope's, and not God's Sabbath. And all we were required to do, was to give up God's Sabbath, and keep the Pope's, and then we should have the mark of the Beast, and of his Image.

In the time of trouble, we all fled from the cities and villages,[58] but were pursued by the wicked, who entered the houses of the saints with the sword. They raised the sword to kill us, but it broke, and fell, as powerless as a straw. Then we all cried day and night for deliverance, and the cry came up before God.[59] The

---

[53] Hosea 6:2, 3.
[54] Ezekiel 7:10-19. 2 Esdras 15:5-27.
[55] 2 Esdras 16:68-74.
[56] Revelation 13:15-17.
[57] Revelation 13:18.
[58] Ezekiel 7:15, 16. Luke 17:30-36. See Campbell's Translation.
[59] Luke 18:7, 8.

sun came up, and the moon stood still.[60] The streams ceased to flow.[61] Dark heavy clouds came up, and clashed against each other.[62] But there was one clear place of settled glory, from whence came the *voice of God* like many waters, which shook the heavens, and the earth.[63] The sky opened and shut, and was in commotion.[64] The [20] mountains shook like a reed in the wind, and cast out ragged rocks all around. The sea boiled like a pot, and cast out stones upon the land.[65] And as God spoke the day and hour of Jesus' coming,[66] and delivered the everlasting covenant to His people,[67] He spoke one sentence, and then paused, while the words were rolling through the earth![68] The Israel of God stood with their eyes fixed upwards, listening to the words as they came from the mouth of Jehovah, and rolled through the earth like peals of loudest thunder! It was awfully solemn. At the end of every sentence, the saints shouted, Glory! Hallelujah! Their countenances were lighted up with the glory of God; and they shone with the glory as Moses' face did when he came down from Sinai. The wicked could not look on them, for the glory.[69] And when the never ending blessing was pronounced on those who had honored God, in keeping His Sabbath holy, there was a mighty shout of victory over the Beast, and over his Image.

Then commenced the jubilee, when the land should rest. I saw the pious slave rise in triumph and victory, and shake

---

[60] Habakkuk 3:11.
[61] 2 Esdras 6:24.
[62] 2 Esdras 15:34, 35.
[63] Joel 3:16. Hebrews 12:25-27.
[64] Revelation 6:14. Matthew 24:29.
[65] Habakkuk 3:8-10. Isaiah 2:19-21.
[66] Ezekiel 12:25. Mark 13:32.
[67] Ezekiel 20:37. Hebrews 12:22-25.
[68] Jeremiah 25:30, 31.
[69] Wisdom of Solomon 5:1-5.

off the chains that bound him, while his wicked master was in confusion, and knew not what to do; for the wicked could not understand the words of the voice of God.[70] Soon appeared the great white cloud.[71] It looked more lovely than ever before. On it sat the Son of Man.[72] At first we did not see Jesus on the cloud, but as it drew near the earth, we could behold his lovely person. This cloud when it first appeared was the Sign of the Son of Man in heaven.[73] The voice of the Son of God called forth the sleeping saints,[74] clothed with a glorious immortality. The living saints were changed in a moment, and caught up with them in the cloudy chariot.[75] It looked all over glorious as it rolled upwards. On either side of the chariot were wings, and beneath it wheels. And as the chariot rolled upwards, the wheels cried Holy, and the wings as they moved, cried Holy, and the retinue of Holy Angels around the cloud cried Holy, Holy, Lord God Almighty. And the saints in the cloud cried Glory, Hallelujah. And the cloudy chariot rolled upwards to the Holy City. Jesus threw open the gates of the Golden City, and led us in.[76] Here we were made welcome, for we had kept the *Commandments* of God," and had a "right to the tree of life."[77]

From your sister in the blessed hope,

E. G. WHITE. [21]

REMARKS. — I do not publish the above vision thinking to add or diminish from the "sure word of prophecy." That will

---

[70] Daniel 12:10.
[71] Revelation 14:14.
[72] Luke 21:27.
[73] Matthew 24:30.
[74] John 5:25-28.
[75] 1 Thessalonians 4:17.
[76] Isaiah 26:2.
[77] Revelation 22:14.

stand the test of men and wreck of worlds! "It is written that man shall not live by bread alone, but by every word of God." Amen.

It is now about two years since I first saw the author, and heard her relate the substance of her visions as she has since published them in Portland (April 6, 1846). Although I could see nothing in them that militated against the word, yet I felt alarmed and tried exceedingly, and for a long time unwilling to believe that it was any thing more than what was produced by a protracted debilitated state of her body.

I therefore sought opportunities in presence of others, when her mind seemed freed from excitement, (out of meeting) to question, and cross question her, and her friends which accompanied her, especially her elder sister, to get if possible at the truth. During the number of visits she has made to New Bedford and Fairhaven since, while at our meetings, I have seen her in vision a number of times, and also in Topsham, Me., and those who were present during some of these exciting scenes know well with what interest and intensity I listened to every word, and watched every move to detect deception, or mesmeric influence. And I thank God for the opportunity I have had with others to witness these things. I can now confidently speak for myself. I believe the work is of God, and is given to comfort and strengthen his "scattered," "torn," and "pealed people," since the closing up of our work for the world in October, 1844. The distracted state of lo, heres! and lo, theres! since that time has exceedingly perplexed God's honest, willing people, and made it exceedingly difficult for such as were not able to expound the many conflicting texts that have been presented to their view. I confess that I have received light and instruction on many passages that I could not before clearly distinguish. I believe her to be a self-sacrificing, honest, willing child of God, and saved, if at all, through her entire obedience to His will.

At a meeting in Fairhaven, 6th of the last month, I saw her have a similar vision, which I then wrote down. It may be said that I send this out to strengthen the argument of my late work on the Sabbath. I do in the sense above stated. Respecting that work I entertain no fears. There is no scriptural argument to move it.

The above vision can be had by application, post paid, to James White, Gorham, Me., or to the editor.

JOSEPH BATES.
Fairhaven, Mass. [22]

Some of our friends have seen this last vision and brother Bates' "remarks," published on a little sheet; but as that sheet cannot be circulated without considerable expense, I have put the vision with Scripture references and the remarks, into this little work, so that they may be widely circulated among the saints.

Those who have received the little sheet will see by referring to Exodus 26:35, that there is a mistake in the 10th and 11th lines from the top of the first column. This mistake is not in the original copy now in my possession, written by the author. I have therefore, corrected this mistake, that I made in hastily copying the vision to send to brother Bates.

It would be gratifying no doubt, to some of the readers of this little work, to know something of the experience and calling of the author of these visions. I have not room to say but very little now, but will make a statement of a few facts well known by the friends in the East. I will first give an extract of a letter from a beloved brother, who has stated I doubt not, his honest views in relation to the visions.

"I cannot endorse sister Ellen's visions as being of divine inspiration, as you and she think them to be; yet I do not suspect the least shade of dishonesty in either of you in this matter. I may perhaps, express to you my belief in the matter, without harm — it will, doubtless, result either in your good or mine. At the same time, I admit the possibility of my being mistaken. I think that what she and you regard as visions from the Lord, are only religious reveries, in which her imagination runs without control upon themes in which she is most deeply interested. While so absorbed in these reveries, she is lost to every thing around her. Reveries are of two kinds, sinful and religious. Hers is the latter. Rosseau's, "a celebrated French infidel," were the former. Infidelity was his theme, and his reveries were infidel. Religion is her theme, and her reveries are religious. In either case, the *sentiments*, in the main, are obtained from previous teaching, or study. I do not by any means think her visions are like some from the devil."

However true this extract may be in relation to reveries, it is *not* true in regard to the visions: for the author *does not* "obtain the sentiments" of her visions "from previous teaching or study." When she received her first vision, Dec. 1844, she and all the band in Portland, Maine, (where her parents then resided) had given up the midnight-cry, and shut door, as being in the past. It was then that the Lord shew her in vision, the error into which she and the band in Portland had fallen. She then related her vision to the band, and about sixty confessed their error, and acknowledged their 7th month experience to be the work of God.

It is well known that many were expecting the Lord to come at the 7th month, 1845. That Christ would then come we firmly believed. A few days before the time passed, I was at Fairhaven, and Dartmouth Mass., with a message on this point of time. At this time, Ellen was with the band at Carver, Mass., where she saw in vision, that we should be disappointed, and that the saints must pass through the "time of Jacob's trouble," which was future. Her view of Jacob's trouble was entirely new to us, as well as herself. At our conference in Topsham, Maine, last Nov., Ellen had a vision of the handy works of God. She was guided to the planets Jupiter, Saturn, and I think one more. After she came out of vision, she could give a clear description of their Moons, etc. It is well known, that she knew nothing of astronomy, and could not answer one question in relation to the planets, before she had this vision. [23]

The Temple of God

"AND the temple of God was opened in heaven and there was seen in his temple the ark of his testament:" — Revelation 11:19.

The Temple of God in which is the ark of his testament, is *in* heaven. St. Paul while in vision, was caught up to the third heaven, or paradise which we believe is the New Jerusalem. The word heaven, is applied to other places beside the New Jerusalem, see Genesis 1:8 and 17; Revelation 14:6. But as they do not contain God's Temple, I must believe that the heaven *in* which is the Temple of God, is the New Jerusalem. Old Jerusalem, and its Temple were types of the New Jerusalem, and God's Temple which is in it. The ark containing the tables of stone, on which God wrote the ten commandments with his own finger, were put into the Holiest. When John had a view of the opening of the New Jerusalem Temple, he saw the ark in the same place in the antitype, that it was in the type.

Therefore it is clear that Old Jerusalem, its Temple, and the furniture of that Temple, have distinct antitypes in Paradise. That Paradise was taken up from the earth after the fall of man, is plain, as there is no such place on the earth which answers the description of it given by Moses. — Genesis 3:23, 24. Also, the prophet says: "Behold, the time shall come, that these tokens which I have told thee shall come to pass, and the Bride shall appear, and she coming forth shall be seen, that *now is withdrawn from the earth*. — 2 Esdras 7:26. The foundations, walls, and gates, of the New Jerusalem, have certainly been formed in Paradise, since Old Jerusalem was built: if not, then the New, is older than the Old. Abraham by faith looked for this City "which hath foundations;" but he did not expect to find it, until the faithful were raised. The Temple of Old Jerusalem was built purposely for the Old Covenant worship. The Temple, or Sanctuary of New Jerusalem, of which Christ is a minister, the Lord pitched and not man, purposely for the New Covenant worship. Therefore, when Christ has finished his ministry in the Heavenly Sanctuary, and has redeemed his people, there will be no more use for the New Jerusalem Temple, than there was for the Temple at Old Jerusalem, after Jesus had nailed the ceremonial law to the cross. John had a view of the Holy City when it shall come down, Revelation 21:10, at the close of the 1000 years, Revelation 20:7-9, and said, "And I saw no temple therein: for the Lord God Almighty and the Lamb are the temple of it — Revelation 21:22. He does not tell us what had become of it; but his saying that he saw no Temple therein at that time, indicates that he had seen one there before. The Holy City is called the Tabernacle of God, Revelation 21:3; Isaiah 33:20; but it is not called so, until it is situated on the New Earth. The City is also called the Temple of God, Revelation 17:15; but not until the saints are raised, and gathered up into the City, where they will serve God "day and night." Then the Holy City alone, will be the Tabernacle, or Temple of God.

THE JUDGMENT

"WHEN the Son of man shall come in his glory, and all the holy angels with him, then shall he sit upon the throne of his glory: And before him shall be gathered all nations: and he shall separate them one from another, as a shepherd divideth his sheep from the goats: And he shall set the sheep on his right hand, but the goats on the left. Matthew 25:31-33. [24]

This scripture evidently points out the most important events of the day of Judgment. That day will be 1000 years long. — 2 Peter 3:7.8. The event which will introduce the Judgment day, will be the coming of the Son of Man, to raise the sleeping saints, and to change those that are alive at that time.

The second event, will be the King's sitting "upon the throne of his glory." The King will not sit upon the throne of his glory, until those who have followed him are raised, and sit upon the thrones of Judgment with him. — Matthew 19:28. John saw in Vision, the length of time that Christ, and the saints would set on the thrones of Judgment, and has written: "And I saw thrones, and they sat upon them, and judgment was given unto them: and I saw the souls of them that were beheaded for the witness of Jesus, and for the word of God, and which had not worshipped the beast, neither his image, neither had received his mark upon their foreheads, or in their hands; and they lived and reigned with Christ a THOUSAND YEARS," Revelation 20:4. The third event, will be the gathering of all nations before the King, in their separate places. All nations cannot be thus gathered, until the end of the 1000 years, when the wicked dead will be raised, and gathered up around the Holy City. The saints will then be in the City, and the wicked out side of it. All nations will then be before him.

The fourth event, will be the delivering of the sentence by the King. His sentence upon the whole host of Gog and Magog, will be, "Depart from me, ye cursed, into everlasting fire, prepared for the devil and his angels," Matthew 25:41. If this is not the final sentence of the judgement on the wicked, I think we shall not find it in the bible. Therefore the wicked are not sentenced before Christ comes; but they will bear their sentence after they are raised, at the close of the 1000 years.

It is not necessary that the final sentence should be given before the first resurrection, as some have taught; for the names of the saints are written in heaven, and Jesus, and the angels will certainly know who to raise, and gather to the New Jerusalem. The fifth event, will be the execution of the final judgment. Some have taken the ground, that the 1000 years will be taken up, in executing the judgment on the wicked: but this cannot be; for the man of sin is to be destroyed with the brightness of Christ's second coming: therefore the wicked are to remain silent in the dust, all through the 1000 years. How can the judgment be executed on the wicked, before they are raised? It is certainly impossible. John saw the wicked, all raised and gathered up around "the camp of the saints," at the end of the 1000 years. He also saw fire come down "from God, out of heaven," which devoured them. This will be the execution of the final judgment on all the wicked.

God executed his judgments on the wicked, in the days of Lot, and Noah, and at the destruction of Jerusalem, and will execute his judgments on the living wicked, at the pouring out of the seven last plagues; but the pouring out of all these judgments cannot be the final execution of the judgment. That will be at the second death. Then God will make all things new. Then shall the King say unto them on his right hand, Come ye blessed of my Father, inherit the kingdom prepared for you from the foundation of the world." — Matthew 25:34. Then God will have a clear Universe; for the Devil, and his angels, and all the wicked, will be burnt up "root and branch."

JAMES WHITE.

This Pamphlet can be had by application, post paid, to the subscriber. My Post Office address is Gorham, Me. [25]

APPENDIX

ELLEN G. WHITE STATEMENTS
NOT REPRINTED

THE reader will have observed that three communications from the pen of Mrs. E. G. White were included in *A Word to the "Little Flock."*

First, there is the letter appearing on pages 11 and 12, addressed to Eli Curtis, in reply to his request for Mrs. White's comments on his prophetic positions as presented in articles in the *Day-Dawn*. In this letter Mrs. White refers to his views on such points as the two resurrections, the Holy City, the cleansing of the sanctuary, etc. This published letter was never reprinted, as the fuller presentation of her views on these subjects obviated the necessity of its being repeated.

The second communication from Mrs. White, found on pages 14-18, is an account of her first vision under the title, "To the Remnant Scattered Abroad." This was written December 20, 1845, as a personal letter to Enoch Jacobs, and was first published by the recipient in The Day-Star, January 24, 1846. Then on April 6, 1846, it was reprinted in broadside form by James White and H. S. Gurney. The statement as it appears in *A Word to the "Little Flock,"* with the exception of minor editorial changes and added scripture references, is identical with the full account of the vision as first printed.

It may be of interest to note that Mrs. White states in a postscript of her letter to Mr. Jacobs, that this account "was not written for publication," and commenting later she wrote, "Had I for once thought it was to be spread before the many readers of your paper, I should have been more particular." — E. G. Harmon, in The Day-Star, March 14, 1846.

The third Ellen G. White communication, occupying pages 18-20, is a reprint of a letter addressed to Joseph Bates, presenting an account of a vision which was given April 7, 1847, in which Mrs. White was shown the most holy place in the heavenly sanctuary, and was then carried into the future and viewed scenes connected with the conflicts and victory of the church. This was first published in broadside form by Elder Bates accompanied by his remarks found on page 21 of *A Word to the "Little Flock."* Scripture references were also added by James White to this third E. G. White communication as it went into print in this pamphlet.

THE FIRST E. G. WHITE BOOK

I N August, 1851, her first book, *A Sketch of the Christian Experience and Views of Ellen G. White*, was published at Saratoga Springs, New York. Among the articles which comprise this work of sixty-four pages are the last two just referred to, which appeared in *A Word to the "Little Flock"* — the first E. G. White vision and the letter to Elder Bates. See *Early Writings*, 13-20; 32-35.

Introducing her first vision as presented in this book, Mrs. White stated, "Here I will give the view which was first published [20] in 1846. In this view I saw only a very few of the events of the future. More recent views have been more full. I shall therefore leave out a portion and prevent repetition." — A Sketch of the Christian Experience and Views of Ellen G. White, 9.

Thus, in the first edition of the first E. G. White book, purporting to be only a "sketch," Mrs. White informed her readers that she was not including all of that which had appeared in earlier published accounts of these visions. A fuller presentation of scenes regarding which but very brief reference has been made in her first visions was given in later chapters of the book, and was set forth by her as the reason for these omissions. We offer two illustrations of this.

Near the center of page 16 of *A Word to the "Little Flock"* is found a statement describing the temple in heaven and that which was viewed by Mrs. White in this temple. This statement is one which was omitted when she prepared the matter for her first book, for it is a close repetition in many respects of the description given on page 18, now found on pages 32 and 33 of *Early Writings.*

On page 19 of *A Word to the "Little Flock"* appears a short paragraph dealing with the "mark of the beast." This paragraph also was omitted by Mrs. White, but we find an entire chapter devoted to this subject in *Early Writings,* 64-67.

The scripture references which appear in the E. G. White communications in *A Word to the "Little Flock"* were inserted by James White. With these are six references to Second Esdras of the Apocrypha. James White assumed the full responsibility for the insertion of all these references, as has been noted by his statement appearing at the bottom of page 13, and they constitute no part of Mrs. White's account.

It will also be observed that in the center of page 19, in connection with the statement regarding the beast and the image beast, the number "666" is found inserted in marks of parenthesis as are the letters referring to the scripture references. The fact that this number appears in parenthesis indicates clearly that it was not a part of the vision, but was inserted by Joseph Bates, the first publisher, as were the scripture references by James White, and reflects the view held by him at that time.

In addition to Mrs. White's brief 1851 statement, referred to above, as to why omissions were made when her first book was published, she, in 1883, wrote at length dealing with most of these omitted portions. Her explanation follows.

MRS. WHITE'S EXPLANATION

"My attention has recently been called to a sixteen-page pamphlet published by----of Marlon, Iowa, entitled *Comparison of the Early Writings of Mrs. White With Later Publications.* The writer states that portions of my earlier visions, as first printed, have been suppressed in the work recently published under the title *Early Writings of Mrs. E. G. White*, and he conjectures as a reason for such suppression that these passages teach doctrines now repudiated by us as a people. [27]

"He also charges us with willful deception in representing *Early Writings* as a complete republication of my carliest views, with only verbal changes from the original work.

"Before I notice separately the passages which are said to have been omitted, it is proper that several facts be stated. When my earliest views were first published in pamphlet form [*A Word to the "Little Flock"*], the edition was small, and was soon sold. This was in a few years followed by a larger book, *The Christian Experience and Views of Mrs. E. G. White*, printed in 1851, and containing much additional matter.

"In our frequent change of location in the earlier history of the publishing work, and then in almost incessant travel as I have labored from Maine to Texas, from Michigan to California — and I have crossed the plains no less than seventeen times

— I lost all trace of the first published works. [1] When it was decided to publish *Early Writings* at Oakland, last fall, we were obliged to send to Michigan to borrow a copy of *Experience and Views*. And in doing this we supposed that we had obtained an exact copy of the earliest visions as first published. This we reprinted, as stated in preface to *Early Writings*, with only verbal changes from the original work.

"And here I will pause to state that any of our people having in their possession a copy of any or all of my first views, as published prior to 1851, will do me a great favor if they will send them to me without delay. I promise to return the same as soon as a copy can be produced.

"So far from desiring to withhold anything that I have ever published, I would feel great satisfaction in giving to the public every line of my writings that has ever been printed....

---

[1] The Day-Star, January 24 and March 14, 1846. Broadsides, April 6, 1846, and April 7, 1847, and *A Word to the "Little Flock."*

OMITTED STATEMENTS

"THE first quotation mentioned by ----- is from a pamphlet of twenty-four pages published in 1847, entitled *A Word to the 'Little Flock.'* Here are the lines omitted in *Experience and Views*:

"'It was just as impossible for them [those that gave up their faith in the '44 movement] to get on the path again and go to the city as all the wicked world which God had rejected. They fell all the way along the path one after another.' [Page 14.]

"I will give the context, that the full force of the expressions may be clearly seen:

"'While praying at the family altar, the Holy Ghost fell on me, and I seemed to be rising higher and higher, far above the dark world. I turned to look for the Advent people in the world, but could not find them — when a voice said to me, "Look again, and look a little higher." At this I raised my eyes and saw a straight and narrow path, cast up high above the world. On this path the Advent people were travelling to the city, which was at the farther end of the path. They had a bright light set up behind them at the first end of the path, which an angel told me was the Midnight Cry. This light shone all along the path, and gave light for their feet so they might not stumble. And if they kept their eyes fixed on Jesus, who was just before them, leading them to the City, they were safe. But soon some grew weary, and they said the City was a great way off, and they expected to have entered it before. Then Jesus would encourage them by raising His glorious right arm, and from His arm came a glorious light which waved over the Advent band, and they shouted Hallelujah. Others rashly denied the light behind them, and said that it was not God that had led them out so far. The light behind them went out leaving their feet in perfect darkness, and they stumbled and got their eyes off the mark and lost sight of Jesus, and fell off the path down in the dark and wicked world below." [28]

"Now follows the passage said to be in the original work, but not found in *Experience and Views* or in *Early Writings*:

"'It was just as impossible for them [those that gave up their faith in the '44 movement] to get on the path again and go to the City, as all the wicked world which God had rejected. They fell all the way along the path one after another.'

"It is claimed that these expressions prove the shut door doctrine, and that this is the reason of their omission, in later editions. But in fact they teach only that which has been and is still held by us as a people, as I shall show.

THE SHUT DOOR DEFINED

"FOR a time after the disappointment in 1844, I did hold in common with the Advent body, that the door of mercy was then forever closed to the world. This position was taken before my first vision was given me. It was the light given me of God that corrected our error, and enabled us to see the true position.

"I am still a believer in the shut door theory, but not in the sense in which we at first employed the term or in which it is employed by my opponents.

"There was a shut door in Noah's day. There was at that time a withdrawal of the Spirit of God from the sinful race that perished in the waters of the flood. God Himself gave the shut door message to Noah:

"'My Spirit shall not always strive with man, for that he also is flesh: yet his days shall be an hundred and twenty years.'

"There was a shut door in the days of Abraham. Mercy ceased to plead with the inhabitants of Sodom, and all but Lot with his wife and two daughters, were consumed by the fire sent down from heaven.

"There was a shut door in Christ's day. The Son of God declared to the unbelieving Jews of that generation, 'Your house is left unto you desolate.'

"Looking down the stream of time to the last days, the same infinite power proclaimed through John:

"'These things saith He that is holy, He that is true, He that hath the key of David, He that openeth, and no man shutteth; and shutteth, and no man openeth.'"

"I was shown in vision, and I still believe, that there was a shut door in 1844. All who saw the light of the first and second angel's messages and rejected that light, were left in darkness. And those who accepted it and received the Holy Spirit which attended the proclamation of the message from heaven, and who afterward renounced their faith and pronounced their experience a delusion, thereby rejected the Spirit of God, and it no longer pleaded with them.

"Those who did not see the light, had not the guilt of its rejection. It was only the class who had despised the light from heaven that the Spirit of God could not reach. And this class included, as I have stated, both those who refused to accept the message when it was presented to them, and also those who, having received it, afterward renounced their faith. These might have a form of godliness, and profess to be followers of Christ, but having no living connection with God, they would be taken captive by the delusions of Satan. These two classes are brought to view in the vision, — those who declared the light which they followed, a delusion, and the wicked of the world who, having rejected the light, had been rejected of God. No reference is made to those who had not seen the light, and therefore were not guilty of its rejection.

"In order to prove that I believed and taught the shut door doctrine, Mr.----gives a quotation from the *Review* of June 11, 1861, signed by nine of our prominent members. The quotation reads as follows: [29]

"'Our views of the work before us were then mostly vague and indefinite, some still retaining the idea adopted by the body of Advent believers in 1844 with William Miller at their head, that our work for "the world" was finished and that the message was confined to those of the original Advent faith. So firmly was this believed, that one of our number was nearly refused the message, the individual presenting it having doubts of the possibility of his salvation because he was not in "the '44 move."

"To this I need only to add that in the same meeting in which it was urged that the message could not be given to this brother [J. H. Waggoner], a testimony was given me through vision to encourage him to hope in God and to give his heart fully to Jesus, which he did then and there.

AN UNREASONABLE CONJECTURE

"IN another passage from the book *A Word to the 'Little Flock,'* I speak of scenes upon the earth, and state that I there saw holy men of old, 'Abraham, Isaac, Jacob, Noah, Daniel, and many like them.' [Page 16] Because I speak of having seen these men, our opponents *conjecture* that I then believed in the immortality of the soul, and that having since changed my views upon this point, I found it necessary to suppress that passage. They are as near the truth here as in other conjectures.

"In the year 1844, I accepted the doctrine we now hold, concerning the nonimmortality of the soul, as may be seen by reference to Life Sketches of Ellen G. White, 170, 171 [1880 ed. See also 1915 ed., p. 49; Testimonies for the Church 1:39, 40], and I have never, by voice or pen, advocated any other. Had we suppressed this passage on account of its teaching the immortality of the soul, we would have found it necessary to suppress other passages.

"In relating my first vision, page 13 of *Early Writings* [1882 ed.; present ed., p. 17], I speak of having seen brethren who had but a short time previous fallen asleep in Jesus, and on page 14 [present ed., p. 18] I state that I was shown a great company who had suffered martyrdom for their faith.

"The immortality of the soul is no more taught in the 'suppressed' passage than in the two last cited.

"The fact in the case is, that in these visions I was carried forward to the time when the resurrected saints shall be gathered into the kingdom of God. In the same manner the Judgment, the second coming of Christ, the establishment of the saints upon the new earth have been presented before me. Does anyone suppose that these scenes have yet transpired? My adversaries show the spirit by which they are actuated in thus accusing me of deception on the strength of a mere 'conjecture.'"

A Misquotation

"IN this quotation are also found the words, 'I saw two long golden rods, on which hung silver wires, and on the wires most glorious grapes.'"

"My opponents ridicule 'that weak and childish expression of glorious grapes growing on silver wires, and these wires attached to golden rods."

"What motive impelled the writer of the above to misstate my words? I do not state that grapes were *growing* on silver wires. That which I beheld is described as it appeared to me. It is not to be supposed that grapes were attached to silver wires or golden rods, but that such was the appearance presented. Similar expressions are daily employed by every person in ordinary conversation. When we speak of golden fruit, we are not understood as declaring that the fruit is composed of that precious metal, but simply that it has the appearance of gold. The same rule applied to my words removes all excuse for misapprehension.

THE SEAL OF GOD

"**A**NOTHER 'suppression' reads as follows:

"'Well, bless the Lord, dear brethren and sisters, it is an extra meeting for those who have the seal of the living God.' [Page 17]

"There is nothing in this that we do not still hold. Reference to our published works will show our belief that the living righteous will receive the seal of God prior to the close of probation. Also that these will enjoy special honors, in the kingdom of God.

Renouncing the Sabbath

"THE following passage is said to be omitted from the vision related on pages 25-28 [pp. 32-35, present ed.] of *Early Writings*:

"'And if one believed, and kept the Sabbath, and received the blessing attending it, and then gave it up, and broke the holy commandment, they would shut the gates of the Holy City against themselves, as sure as there was a God that rules in heaven above.' [Page 19]

"Those who have clearly seen and fully accepted the truth upon the fourth commandment and have received the blessing attending obedience, but have since renounced their faith, and dared to violate the law of God, will find if they persist in this path of disobedience, the gates of the city of God closed against them....

"There are two other passages said to be found in my first book, but not given in my later writings. Concerning these I shall only say, when I can obtain a book containing them, so that I can be assured of the correctness of the quotations and can see for myself their connection, I shall be prepared to speak understandingly in regard to them.

"From the beginning of my work, I have been pursued by hatred, reproach, and falsehood. Base imputations and slanderous reports have been greedily gathered up and widely circulated by the rebellious, the formalist, and the fanatic. There are ministers of the so-called orthodox churches traveling from place to place to war against Seventh-day Adventists and they make Mrs. White their textbook. The scoffers of the last days are led on by those ministers professing to be God's watchmen.

"The unbelieving world, the ministers of the fallen churches, and the First-day Adventists are all united in the work of assailing Mrs. White. This warfare has been kept up for nearly forty years, but I have not felt at liberty even to notice their vile speeches, reproaches, and insinuations. And I would not now depart from this custom, were it not that some honest souls may be misled by the enemies of the truth who are so exultantly declaring me a deceiver. In the hope of helping the minds of the honest, I make the statements that I do." — *Ellen G. White MS 4, 1883.*

Adventist Pioneer Library

For more information, visit:
www.APLib.org

or write to:
apl@netbox.com

www.ingramcontent.com/pod-product-compliance
Lightning Source LLC
Chambersburg PA
CBHW071506070426
42452CB00041B/2383